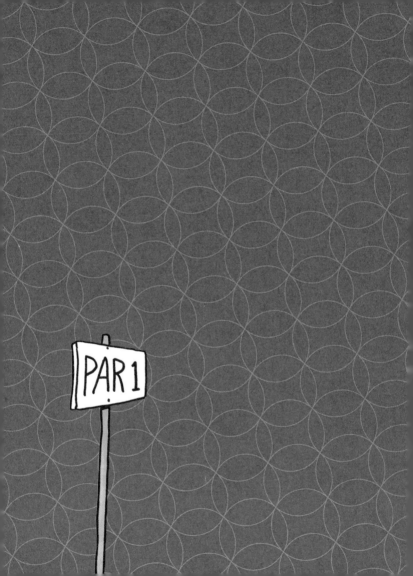

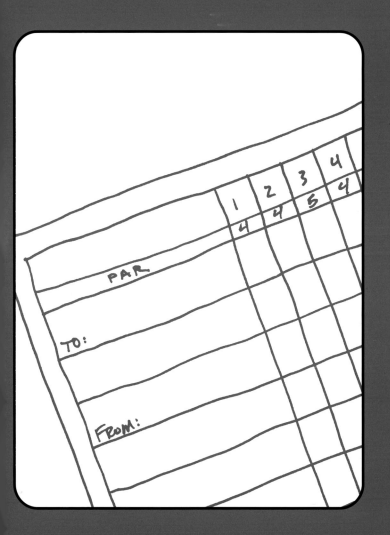

When coffee shop owners manage pro shops

"Do you, Margaret, take this man, his golf clubs, his golf buddies, their caddies, wives, and friends to be your lawfully wedded husband?"

Indoor Range

"It's amazing what men will do if you just tell them it will improve their golf game."

"Don't eat the ones holding sticks,
they're hard to swallow."

The "Missing Links" Course

"I said golf *tees* - not *tease*."

"Go back to the pitchfork, I think it works better."

"Why yes, we do have a reservation."

"And the winner of this year's longest drive
goes to a visitor."

"Oh, they look tame, Bobby. Wait 'til one of them
tries to pick up the other guy's golf ball."

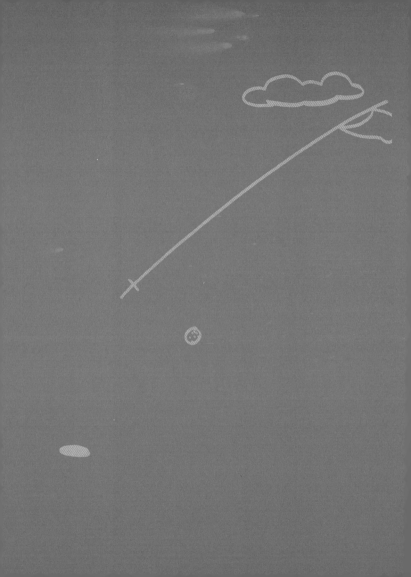

"Dear Omri, the weather in Thebes is great and the golf even better. Wish you were here. Say hello to the kids."

"My wife? Oh, she's at home. I only had two tickets."

First published in the United States by
Tony Potter Publishing Ltd, Haywards Heath,
West Sussex RH17 5HX

This edition published in 2005 by
POWERFRESH Limited
Unit 3 Everdon Park
Heartlands Industrial Estate
Daventry NN11 8YJ
Telephone 01327 871 777
Facsimile   01327 879 222
E Mail info@powerfresh.co.uk

Printed in Singapore

ISBN   1-904967-12-4

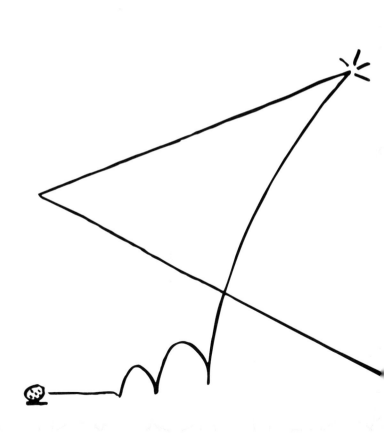

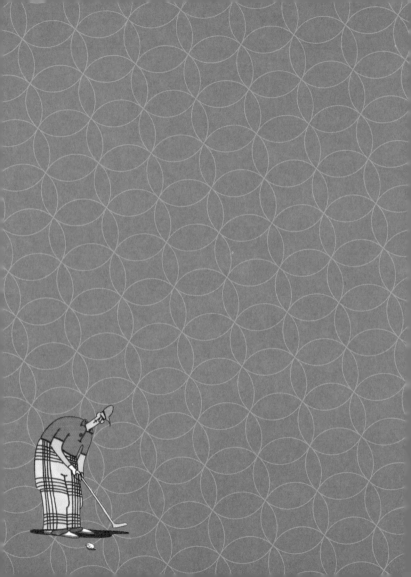